ULTIMATE SLIME

D0102993

DISCARDED

ULTIMATE SLIME

ALYSSA JAGAN

Totally Borax Free!

DIY Tutorials for Crunchy Slime, Fluffy Slime, Fishbowl Slime, and More Than **100** Other Oddly Satisfying Recipes and Projects

QUARRY

Brimming with creative inspiration, how-to projects, and useful information to enrich your everyday life, Quarto Knows is a favorite destination for those pursuing their interests and passions. Visit our site and dig deeper with our books into your area of interest: Quarto Creates, Quarto Cooks, Quarto Homes, Quarto Lives, Quarto Drives, Quarto Explores, Quarto Gifts, or Quarto Kids.

© 2017 Quarto Publishing Group USA Inc.

First Published in 2017 by Quarry Books, an imprint of The Quarto Group, 100 Cummings Center, Suite 265-D, Beverly, MA 01915, USA. T (978) 282-9590 F (978) 283-2742 QuartoKnows.com

All rights reserved. No part of this book may be reproduced in any form without written permission of the copyright owners. All images in this book have been reproduced with the knowledge and prior consent of the artists concerned, and no responsibility is accepted by producer, publisher, or printer for any infringement of copyright or otherwise, arising from the contents of this publication. Every effort has been made to ensure that credits accurately comply with information supplied. We apologize for any inaccuracies that may have occurred and will resolve inaccurate or missing information in a subsequent reprinting of the book.

Quarry Books titles are also available at discount for retail, wholesale, promotional, and bulk purchase. For details, contact the Special Sales Manager by email at specialsales@quarto.com or by mail at The Quarto Group, Attn: Special Sales Manager, 401 Second Avenue North, Suite 310, Minneapolis, MN 55401, USA.

10 9 8 7 6 5 4 3 2

ISBN: 978-1-63159-425-0

Digital edition published in 2017

Library of Congress Cataloging-in-Publication Data available

Design: Kathie Alexander
Cover Image: Glenn Scott Photography
Page Layout: Kathie Alexander
Photography: Alyssa Jagan, except Glenn Scott Photography pages 3, 10, 11, 38, 39, 54, 55; and Amanda De Matos, page 111
Illustration: shutterstock.com

Printed in China

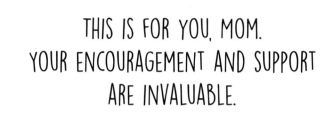

THIS IS FOR YOU, MOM.
YOUR ENCOURAGEMENT AND SUPPORT
ARE INVALUABLE.

ACKNOWLEDGMENTS

In all honesty. I'm unsure of where to begin thanking all the people who have supported me through this whirlwind. My sincerest gratitude to:

- Amanda De Matos, who has been my cheerleader throughout this whole process. Thank you for teaching me how to take photos that aren't blurry.

- All my friends, especially Mansi Chugh, the Lane to my Rory and the Cristina to my Meredith. Thank you for dealing with my sleep-deprived brain and for the never-ending words of encouragement.

- Every single one of my teachers and mentors, most importantly Ms. Welbourn and Ms. Cullen. All of you inspire me to learn more and do more.

- The whole team at Quarto: Marissa Giambrone, Diane Naughton, Lara Neel, John Gettings, Mary Ann Hall, Winnie Prentiss, David Breuer, Ken Fund, and countless others. Thank you for all the time and energy you've put into making my dreams a reality.

- Joy Aquilino, the best editor I could have asked for. You deserve an award for your patience and dedication.

- My amazing family—my mother, father, grandparents, and sister. Thank you for the late night runs to the store for slime supplies, letting me take all the airtight containers in the house that I could find, and being there for me no matter what. I couldn't have done any of this without you guys.

- Lastly—thank you, Cierra Jagan, for your computer charger.

CONTENTS

INTRODUCTION

Slime is not a new thing for many of us, whether we made it in science class or with our parents when we were younger.

Well, slime is back and bigger than ever!

The trend began in the summer of 2016, spreading like wildfire through social media. I began sharing videos of my slime in late August and have since gained a following of over half a million. Slime has become a hobby and creative outlet for many people. I'm constantly asked how to make slime, and I could never find a comprehensive guide to point people to, so I decided to write this book.

If you follow the instructions, you'll find it's fairly simple to make slime. I cover a few different options for activating slime, which means to make the ingredients in the slime come together to create the signature "slimey" texture. All the recipes in this book are borax-free. While I typically use borax solution as an activator, because this book is for kids, many of whom are beginner slimers and some of whom might be sensitive to borax, I wanted to share alternatives. It's your and

your parents' decision to choose which activator you would like to use—please research and talk to your parents about this before making slime so together you can make an informed decision.

Keep in mind that a chemical reaction is occurring when slime is made, regardless of which activator you use. Also, make sure that you are not allergic to any of the materials used in slime making.

Once you've mastered basic slimes, you can customize them using your imagination. This book offers some interesting ideas of what you can do with your slime, but you're also encouraged to experiment using your creativity.

Please post videos and photos of your creations on Instagram and YouTube with the hashtag #craftyslimecreations so we can see slime inspired by the book or new and creative ways you have used slime. I've connected with lots of great people by making slime and sharing it on social media—I'm sure you will too!

MAKING SLIME SAFELY: A NOTE FOR ADULTS

- **Always supervise children closely** when they're working with slime or any of its ingredients. Handle all products used to make slime carefully.

- **Do not use a product if you or a child has a sensitivity to it, and discontinue the use of any product if you or a child has an adverse reaction to it.**

- **Never eat slime** and *never* let children put slime or any of its ingredients in their mouths.

- **Always label slime so it won't be mistaken for food.** It's especially important to label food replicas that are made with slime to avoid having someone mistake them for food.

- **Always store slime out of the reach of children,** especially young children and pets.

- **Do not prepare slime on surfaces or in areas used to prepare or serve food.**

- **Always use disposable bowls and utensils to make slime.** Or, set aside a set of bowls and utensils that you use only for slime making and never reuse them for food preparation or for bathing.

- **Avoid getting slime on exposed skin or clothing.**

- **Always have adequate ventilation** when making slime.

- **Always make and store slime at room temperature.** Never freeze or heat slime.

- **When throwing slime away, make sure you're in compliance with local, state, and federal laws** for disposing its ingredients.

- **After handling slime, always wash your hands thoroughly** with soap and water.

SLIME BASICS

THIS CHAPTER IS THE FOUNDATION FOR EVERYTHING ELSE IN THIS BOOK. THESE BASIC RECIPES AND TIPS AND TRICKS ARE ESSENTIAL FOR MAKING SLIME SUCCESSFULLY.

WHAT YOU'LL NEED

This section lists the essential ingredients for making slime: a glue base, an activator, and some optional add-ins to adjust the texture.

It's important that you have an adult help you so they can show you how to handle the materials and work with them safely. See Making Slime Safely on page 9 for more information.

Polyvinyl Acetate (PVA) Glue

White or clear PVA glue is used as the base in all the recipes in this book. Make sure the one you use is non-toxic. If you're unsure whether a glue is PVA, test it on scrap paper: PVA glue always dries clear.

I use Elmer's School Glue, which is white and opaque (pronounced oh-PAKE, which means you can't see through it), and Elmer's Clear School Glue, which is colorless and clear. Each recipe in this book tells you which type you need. For example, Fishbowl Slime (see page 42) must be made with clear glue, but you can only get the creamy texture of Soft Serve Slime (page 78) with white glue.

Activators

The activator is the most important slime ingredient. Adding just the right amount of one of these mixtures or products to the glue "activates" its polymer (plasticlike) molecules so they become stretchy.

Baking soda and contact lens solution. Using these products together makes a good activator. The contact lens solution must contain boric acid or buffered saline. Renu Fresh Multipurpose Solution is the one I use. While other activators may make clear slime cloudy, the baking soda + contact lens solution makes a good clear slime.

Liquid laundry detergent. A liquid laundry detergent containing boric acid or a borate ion, such as Tide Free and Gentle, is yet another product that can be used to activate slime. Note that some people don't like to use liquid laundry detergent as an activator because the slime will smell just like the detergent.

Liquid starch. This type of starch, such as Sta-Flo, can also be used as a slime activator.

I encourage you and your parents to do research and perhaps try a couple of these options so you can make your own decision about which activator to use.

Optional Add-Ins

Adding one of these ingredients to a basic slime mixture will affect its texture in a slightly different way. Before you add any personal care products—foaming hand soap or facial cleanser, lotion, or shaving cream—make sure you like the product's color and scent because it will affect your slime. For example, if your hand soap is green and pear-scented, your slime will have a green tint and smell like pears. If I'm adding more than one product, I like their scents to match. You can also use unscented products and either leave your slime unscented or add a fragrance oil (see page 25).

- **Cornstarch.** This is used to thicken slime so it holds its shape and also gives it a matte finish. Some slimers use baby powder as a thickener, but I don't find that it works well.

- **Foaming hand soap.** This product can't be used by itself as an activator, but it does help activate and bring the slime together, making it smoother and stretchier. Be sure that the hand soap is the foaming type; otherwise, it won't work. The dispenser/pump is the most important thing as it gives the soap a foamy texture.

- **Foaming facial cleanser.** This is used to make fluffy slime. The effect lasts for 1 to 2 weeks, quite a bit longer than shaving cream (see below). The brand I use is Clean & Clear Foaming Facial Cleanser.

- **Glycerin.** This is added to clear slime to make it stretchier. Do not use glycerin if you plan to add beads or other small elements to the slime, as it will cause them to fall out.

- **Lotion.** Adding lotion also makes slime stretchier. You can use any type of lotion.

- **Shaving cream.** This also makes slime fluffy, but it will deflate after 2 to 4 days. Make sure to use a foaming shaving cream.

- **Baby oil.** This is used to give extra gloss to white glue slime. Adding it to clear slime will make it cloudy.

MAKING SLIME WITHOUT BORAX

There have been some concerns about borax, which can be used to activate slime, but it's not the only option. Instead, you can use liquid laundry detergent, liquid starch, or a mixture of contact lens solution and baking soda. I've made slime with these three alternatives and they all work well.

Refer to the recipes for Basic White Glue Slime (page 14) and Basic Clear Glue Slime (page 16) for details about how much of each activator should be used. *Always use only one type of activator to make each batch of slime.*

BASIC WHITE GLUE SLIME

THIS IS AN EASY RECIPE FOR MAKING GLOSSY SLIME. YOU CAN ADAPT IT TO MAKE A VARIETY OF OTHER, MORE ADVANCED SLIMES.

WHAT YOU'LL NEED

Slime-Making Equipment

Large bowl

Mixing tool (spoon, spatula, or stir stick)

Measuring cups and spoons

Airtight container

Ingredients

1 cup (250 ml) white PVA glue (such as Elmer's School Glue)

An activator (see chart below for details)

Approximately ½ cup (125 ml) foaming hand soap

Optional

Color additive

1–3 drops of fragrance oil

HOW MUCH ACTIVATOR DO I NEED?

It depends on which activator you choose! See the recommended amounts to the right. **Add no more than 2 tablespoons (30 ml) of activator at a time, and then stir well. Check the consistency of the slime before adding more.** The amount of activator you add will affect the consistency; you can adjust it to a consistency you like, or one you want for a specific recipe.

If you add too much activator, your slime will become hard, but if you don't add enough, it will be too sticky.

If you make a mistake and need to fix your slime, go to the Troubleshooting section on page 18.

Remember—only use one type of activator for each batch of slime!

Activator	Recommended Amount
Liquid laundry detergent	5 to 7 tablespoons (75 to 105 ml)
Liquid starch (such as Sta-Flo)	6 to 8 tablespoons (90 to 120 ml)
Baking soda + contact lens solution	Add 1 tablespoon (15 ml) baking soda to the slime, then add 1 to 2 tablespoons (15 to 30 ml) contact lens solution. Renu Fresh Multipurpose Solution works well; if you use other brands, you may need to add a lot more.

SLIME BASICS

1.

Place the glue in a large bowl. Add foaming hand soap to the glue (see A). If you want, add color and/or fragrance oil (see pages 24 and 25 for some options). Mix thoroughly.

A.

Yield:
Approximately
14 fluid ounces
(440 ml)

2.

Add your activator to the glue in small amounts, no more than 2 tablespoons (30 ml) at a time (see B). See the guidelines opposite for the recommended amounts of each type of activator—*be sure to add only one type of activator to each batch of slime.*

B.

3.

Once the mixture is slightly sticky, start to knead the slime (see C). Dip your fingers in a little activator before kneading so less slime will stick to your hands. Playing with slime is the best way to mix it fully and get the best possible texture.

C.

4.

Store the finished slime in an airtight container so it doesn't dry out. For the best glossy texture, let the slime sit for 2 to 4 days.

SLIME BASICS

RECIPES AND PROJECTS MADE WITH BASIC WHITE GLUE SLIME

BASIC CLEAR GLUE SLIME

THIS IS A SIMPLE RECIPE FOR MAKING BASIC CLEAR SLIME. MANY OTHER RECIPES USE IT, SO IT'S DEFINITELY A SLIME YOU'LL WANT TO MASTER. FOR TIPS AND TRICKS ON CREATING COMPLETELY CLEAR SLIME, CHECK OUT THE RECIPE ON PAGE 72.

WHAT YOU'LL NEED

Slime-Making Equipment

Large bowl
Measuring cups and spoons
Mixing tool (spoon, spatula, or stir stick)
Airtight container

Ingredients

1 cup (250 ml) clear PVA glue (such as Elmer's Clear Glue)
An activator (see chart below)

Optional

Color additive (see page 24)
1 to 3 drops fragrance oil (please note that this may make clear glue–based slimes cloudy)
1 teaspoon (5 ml) glycerin

Yield: Approximately 14 fluid ounces (440 ml)

HOW MUCH ACTIVATOR DO I NEED?

As with Basic White Glue Slime (see page 14), the amount of activator you need for Basic Clear Glue Slime depends on which activator you choose! See the recommended amounts below. **Add no more than 2 tablespoons (30 ml) of activator at a time, then stir well.** Check the consistency of the slime before adding more. The amount of activator you add will affect the consistency; you can adjust it to a consistency you like, or one you want for a specific recipe.

If you add too much activator, your slime will become hard, but if you don't add enough it will be too sticky.

If you make a mistake and need to fix your slime, go to the Troubleshooting section on page 18.

Remember—only use one type of activator for each batch of slime!

Activator	Recommended Amount
Liquid laundry detergent	4 to 6 tablespoons (60 to 90 ml)
Liquid starch (such as Sta-Flo)	5 to 7 tablespoons (75 to 105 ml)
Baking soda + contact lens solution	Add 1 tablespoon (15 ml) baking soda to the slime and then add 1 to 3 tablespoons (15 to 45 ml) contact lens solution. Renu Fresh Multipurpose Solution works well; if you use other brands, you may need to add a lot more.

SLIME BASICS

1.

Place the glue in a large bowl. Add coloring and/or fragrance oil if you like, but note that some fragrance oils may make your slime cloudy. Add 1 teaspoon (5 ml) of glycerin (see A), but only if you're not going to include any add-ins. The glycerin will make the slime stretchier but it won't be able to hold things. For the clearest possible slime, mix slowly. Feel free to mix quickly, but you'll need to wait longer for the slime to clear because there will be more bubbles.

2.

Add the activator in small amounts, no more than 2 tablespoons (30 ml) at a time (see B). See the guidelines opposite for the recommended amounts of each type of activator—be sure to add only one type to each batch of slime. Stir the mixture well after adding the activator to make sure you don't add too much. Also, the amount you add will affect the slime's consistency, and you can adjust it to achieve a consistency you like.

3.

Once the mixture is slightly sticky (see C), start to knead the slime. Dip your fingers in the activator before kneading so less slime will stick to your hands. Playing with slime is the best way to mix it fully. Remember to have clean hands when doing this, as anything on your hands will be seen in the clear slime.

4.

Store the finished slime in an airtight container so it doesn't dry out.

RECIPES AND PROJECTS MADE WITH BASIC CLEAR GLUE SLIME

Recipes

Avalanche Slime (page 84)
Bubbly Slime (page 82)
Completely Clear Slime (page 72)
Clear Glue Floam (page 60)
Fishbowl Slime (page 42)

Gem Slime (page 62)
Glitter Bomb (page 52)
Metallic Slime (page 56)
Slushie Slime (page 40)

Projects

Decorative Slime Jars (page 104)
DIY Slime Stress Ball (page 98)
Slime Food Replicas (page 100)

TROUBLESHOOTING

This section addresses the two problems you're most likely to experience when making slime.

Is Your Slime Too Sticky?

Did you leave your slime alone for a few weeks and it liquefied? Do you just have really sticky slime? Simply add activator to fix it! This should fix most sticky slimes.

If just adding activator isn't working, try adding in stiff slime or cornstarch to thicken it.

Keep in mind that some liquefied slimes simply won't activate again and you might just need to throw them out.

Is Your Slime Too Hard or Stiff?

Did you add too much activator? Or play with your slime all day long and now it's ripping apart? Here are some suggestions for fixing it.

For any type of slime, you can try just waiting a few days before trying to fix it. When you first make slime, it will have lots of air bubbles in it from mixing and kneading. These bubbles make slime tear easily. When the bubbles rise and pop, the slime will become stretchier.

If your white glue–based slime still isn't stretchy enough even after waiting a couple of days, add lotion to it. Note that adding lotion to clear glue–based slimes will make them cloudy.

Dipping any type of slime in warm water also works very well, but be careful that the water isn't too hot. Be sure to have an adult help you with this. Also, don't add too much water or your slime might become jiggly or even liquefy!

IF YOUR SLIME IS TOO STICKY (LEFT),
START BY MIXING IN A LITTLE MORE
ACTIVATOR TO CORRECT IT (RIGHT).
IF THAT DOESN'T WORK, TRY ADDING
STIFF SLIME OR CORNSTARCH.

IF YOUR WHITE GLUE—BASED SLIME IS
TOO STIFF (LEFT), TRY ADDING LOTION
AND THEN TAKE IT FROM THERE (RIGHT)!
YOU CAN ALSO TRY TO CORRECT ANY
TYPE OF SLIME THAT'S TOO STIFF BY
DIPPING IT IN WARM WATER.

STORING SLIME

Slime will dry out if you don't store it properly!

Store your slime in an airtight container if you want it to last a long time. You can use old yogurt or other food containers—just be sure to wash and dry them thoroughly first and to label them so everyone will know that they contain slime.

You can also store slime in resealable bags, but in my experience, this causes the slime to liquefy faster.

Always keep stored slime out of the reach of young children!

EDIBLE SLIME

THIS SLIME IS PERFECT FOR SOMEONE WHO DOESN'T WANT TO USE ACTIVATOR OR IS MAKING SLIME WITH VERY YOUNG CHILDREN WHO MIGHT PUT THE SLIME OR THEIR HANDS IN THEIR MOUTHS WHEN PLAYING WITH SLIME. ALTHOUGH IT'S MADE WITH EDIBLE INGREDIENTS IT SHOULDN'T BE SERVED AS A SNACK.

A.

WHAT YOU'LL NEED

Slime-Making Equipment

Microwave-safe bowl
Mixing tool (spoon, spatula, or stir stick)
Measuring cups and spoons
An airtight container

Ingredients

1 cup (250 ml) marshmallows
¾ cup (180 ml) cornstarch

Optional

Food coloring
½ tsp (2.5 ml) water **or** ½ tsp (2.5 ml) oil
(any kind of cooking oil, such as olive oil, will work)

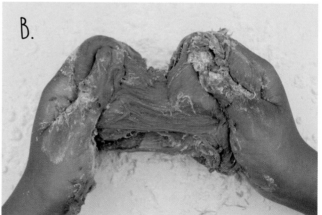

B.

VARIATIONS

Buttery Edible Slime
= Edible Slime + yellow food coloring
Dusty Rose Edible Slime
= Edible Slime + red food coloring
Cake Batter Edible Slime
= Edible Slime + edible sprinkles

SLIME BASICS

C.

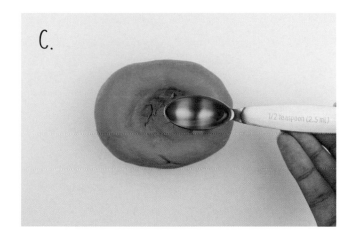

D.

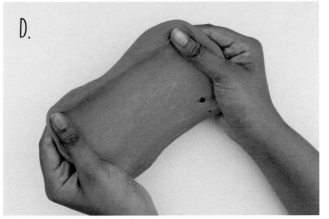

1.

Place the marshmallows in the bowl. Microwave for 30 seconds and then stir. Repeat until the marshmallows are melted. If you like, add food coloring to the melted marshmallows. Mix well.

2.

Stir ½ cup (125 ml) cornstarch into the melted marshmallow mixture (see A).

3.

Once the mixture is slightly sticky, start to knead the slime. Dip your fingers in cornstarch and coat the surface with the remaining ¼ cup (60 ml) of cornstarch before kneading so less slime will stick to your hands and table (see B). Playing with slime is the best way to mix it fully and achieve the best possible texture.

4.

Add water or oil to add stretchiness to your slime (see C). If the slime becomes too sticky, add more cornstarch. Repeat this process until you're happy with the consistency of the slime. Remember that this slime isn't glossy and pokable like regular slime; it's more like a buttery, dough-like slime (see D).

5.

Store your slime in an airtight container so it doesn't dry out. It will last for 1–2 days, but best played with when freshly made.

SAFETY NOTE!

Although this recipe isn't meant to be eaten, if there's any chance your edible slime may be ingested, do **not** use the same tools you use for regular slime-making to make it!

Yield: ⅓ cup (85 g) slime

ADDING COLOR AND DIMENSION

IN THIS CHAPTER, YOU'LL LEARN ABOUT THE DIFFERENT PRODUCTS YOU CAN USE TO GIVE YOUR SLIME AMAZING COLORS AND TEXTURES—FROM PAINTS AND PIGMENTS TO GLITTER, FOAM BEADS, FAKE SNOW, AND MORE! YOU CAN EASILY FIND WHAT YOU NEED IN CRAFT STORES OR ONLINE.

COLORING SLIME

There are many ways to color slime. My favorite way is to use food coloring because it doesn't have a scent. I use the liquid drops, but gel food coloring works as well.

You can use acrylic paint as well. Be careful when using it, though, because it can have an unpleasant smell, and if you use too much, it can dry out your slime.

You can also use pigments, which are colorful powders, to add color to your slime. I use Pearl Ex Pigments for this.

There are also a couple of options for creating metallic colors:

- For clear slime, use pearlescent acrylic paint in a color of your choice.

- If you don't want to buy the metallic versions of many colors, you can add either white pearl metallic paint or iridescent white pigment plus food coloring or acrylic paint. This method works for both white glue or clear glue slimes.

(LEFT) ACRYLIC PAINT, PIGMENT, AND LIQUID OR GEL FOOD COLORING ARE ALL GOOD OPTIONS FOR COLORING SLIME. (ABOVE) A TEAL METALLIC CLEAR GLUE SLIME.

FRAGRANCE OILS

Use fragrance oils that are craft grade. Be sure to use fragrance oils that are safe for your hands. Also, make sure that you don't have a sensitivity to them. Do not use food-grade scented oils, which will spoil your slime.

It's a good idea to start off with a few drops until you are familiar with the intensity of the scent. I like to use a dropper to add the fragrance oil to my slime to avoid pouring out too much. You can try mixing different scents together to make your desired scent.

Keep in mind that adding fragrance oil to clear slime can make it cloudy. It's difficult to know which oils might trigger this because clear slime is very difficult to keep clear-—it can even become cloudy from the natural oils on your hands.

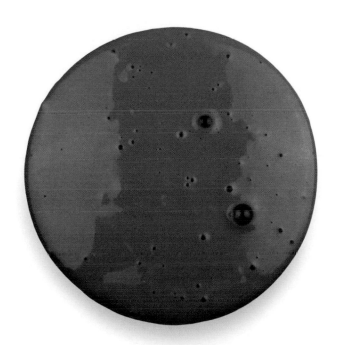

AN ORCHID—COLORED SLIME (LEFT) FEATURING A BLEND OF FLORAL FRAGRANCE OILS.

GLITTER

Glitter is an essential slime add-in. It adds a pop of gorgeous color and texture, especially in clear slime.

There are a few things to keep in mind when working with glitter and slime:

- If you love glitter, it can be tempting to add a lot of it to your slime, but don't add too much or it will fall out of the slime and stick to your hands or surfaces.

- Many types of glitter, including chunky, fine, holographic, and more, all work as slime ingredients. Do not use flake glitters or sequins because they can be sharp.

Glitter in white glue slimes can look clumpy, but it's all about making creative choices. Try adding a chunky black glitter to pink or green white glue slime to make watermelon or kiwi slime. Or try adding black glitter to a mint green–colored white glue slime to make a mint chocolate chip ice cream slime. Use your imagination!

The good news is that all glitter looks good in clear slime! Make a glitter bomb by mixing equal amounts of glitter and sticky clear slime—the slime will be crunchy and colorful. Try adding a couple of different glitters, like holographic silver and blue, to see if their colors complement each other. Consider the color of the slime when choosing the glitter to make sure everything works well together.

SPARKLY GLITTERS IN A VARIETY OF COLORS AND SHAPES (ABOVE) AND A GORGEOUS SLIME MADE WITH THE TWO FINE GLITTERS.

POLYMER CLAY CANES

Polymer clay canes—tiny images made from polymer clay that's been sliced super-thin and then baked—are adorable! They're the perfect thing to add to clear glue slimes. I don't recommend adding canes to white glue slimes because it's hard to see them after they've been mixed in.

Polymer clay cane designs range from simple fruits to intricate characters. You can find them in nail art stores, dollar stores, and online. They're sold already sliced and in logs that you can slice yourself. Personally, I prefer the presliced canes because I can never cut them thin enough. You can also learn to make your own canes. There are lots of how-to books about it.

My favorite recipes to make with canes are food-themed. For example, you can make clear lemon slime with lemon cane slices and yellow coloring or fruit salad floam with a mixture of fruit canes and foam beads.

POLYMER CLAY FRUIT CANES (LEFT) AND A BATCH OF CLEAR STRAWBERRY SLIME.

MICROBEADS

Microbeads are tiny metal balls that are only a few millimeters in diameter. They add a cool texture and a bit of glitz to your slime. Sometimes, I add them to floam for a pop of color. They're also perfect as fake watermelon or kiwi seeds in fruit-themed slimes.

Microbeads can be used in both clear and white glue slimes but are most easily visible in clear glue slimes.

MICROBEADS IN RICH JEWEL TONES (RIGHT) AND A PALE PINK SLIME SPRINKLED WITH MICROBEADS.

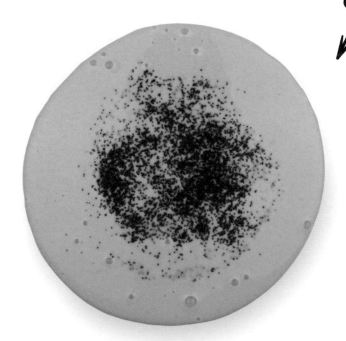

FOAM BEADS

Foam beads come in many different sizes and colors. They are usually made of polystyrene and are between 1 and 10 millimeters in diameter.

The smallest size can be found in travel neck pillows. This is a micro foam bead between 1 and 2 millimeters in diameter. These tend to make a huge mess and are difficult to contain, but they add a great crunchy texture in floam that's very satisfying. Larger sizes are used as beanbag filler.

Some foam beads come in a pack of one color or in a pack with a variety of colors. Sometimes, the colors may rub off on your slime, so take that into account when choosing the base color of your slime.

I use foam beads in Confetti Slime (see page 48), and they also add an interesting texture and color to basic slime.

FOAM BEADS IN THREE DIFFERENT SIZES (LEFT), AND A DARK PURPLE FLOAM MADE WITH MICRO FOAM BEADS.

FISHBOWL BEADS

Fishbowl beads are a disk-shaped plastic vase filler bead. This can be a difficult product to find. Sometimes, the beads have sharp edges, so be careful when using these. I use these to make Fishbowl Slime (see page 42).

FISHBOWL BEADS (ABOVE) AND A GREEN FISHBOWL SLIME.

SLUSHIE SLIME BEADS

Slushie slime beads are similar to fishbowl beads but they have rounded, smooth edges. These beads are used to fill stuffed animals. I make Slushie Slime (see page 40) with these beads.

SLUSHIE SLIME BEADS (ABOVE) AND A ROSE GOLD SLUSHIE SLIME.

SUGAR SLIME BEADS

Sugar slime beads are tiny cylindrical-shaped vase filler beads. They create an interesting texture for slime that's crunchy and very fun to squeeze. I use these to make Sugar Slime (see page 50), which is a modified Fishbowl Slime (see page 42).

SUGAR SLIME BEADS (LEFT)
AND GOLD SUGAR SLIME.

FLOCKING POWDER

Flocking powder is made up of lots of tiny fibers. It adds an interesting, speckled pop of color and fuzzy texture to slime. You can add it to Soft Serve Slime (see page 78) to make it speckled.

FLOCKING POWDER IN THREE BRIGHT COLORS (RIGHT) AND LIGHT GREEN SOFT SERVE SLIME.

FAKE SNOW

Fake snow—the kind that's sprinkled around Christmas decorations—is made of small pieces of plastic. Before you use fake snow, make sure it's made of plastic and not any other material. Also be careful when choosing fake snow because some brands have sharp pieces of plastic and some have large, flimsy pieces. I like the brand FloraCraft. I use this in Cotton Candy Slime (see page 64).

TO MAKE COTTON CANDY
SLIME (LEFT), ADD SOME
FAKE SNOW.

SUPER-ABSORBENT POLYMER (SAP)

Super-absorbent polymer, or SAP, is made from a material that can absorb and retain large amounts of water. As water is added, it fluffs up and increases in size.

SAP can be found in diapers, in water beads, in a type of fake snow that fluffs up, and as SAP powder (sometimes called Instant Snow).

- You can open up an unused diaper and scrape out the small amount of SAP material.

- If you use water beads, you have to soak them in water, crush every bead, and then add them to slime.

- I prefer to use the fake snow that fluffs up when water is added or the SAP powder.

- If you use colored water, then the SAP becomes that color. I use this to make Gem Slime (see page 62).

Regardless of which type you use, be sure to start off with a very tiny amount because SAP may increase to fifty times its volume when water is added!

SUPER—ABSORBENT POLYMER (SAP) IN THREE COLORS (ABOVE) AND BRIGHT RED GEM SLIME.

AIR-DRY CLAY

Air-dry clay changes the texture of your slime and makes it fluffier or denser, depending on the type of clay you use. Some air-dry clays are denser than others, which should be taken into account when deciding which one to use. For example, Crayola Model Magic is dense and will create a thick slime, whereas Delight Air Dry Modeling Compound and Hearty Modeling Clay are not dense and will create a light slime. I typically use Daiso Soft Clay to make Butter Slime (see page 76).

A tip to keep in mind is that some air-dry clays are tougher than others and may need lotion to soften them. All the air-dry clays create an interesting texture, but be sure to experiment with the ratio of air-dry clay to the slime you use. You can also mix different brands of air-dry clay together.

AIR—DRY CLAY IN THREE COLORS (ABOVE) AND BUTTER SLIME AND CLAY SLIME.

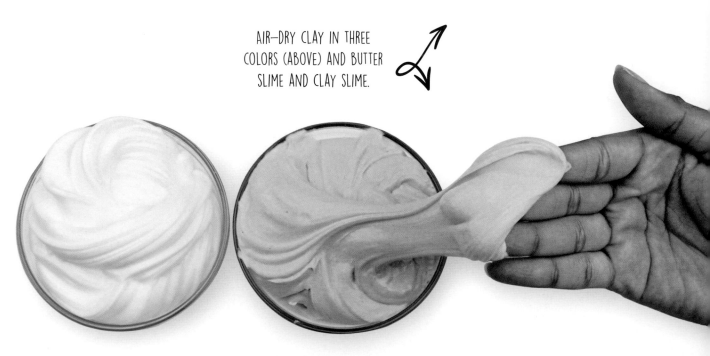

KINETIC SAND AND MAD MATTR

These products, which are used to make Kinetic Slime (page 66), are similar to actual sand but they aren't as messy—and they actually mix better with slime!

Sometimes called indoor play sand or magic sand, Kinetic Sand and Mad Mattr include a substance that makes them feel like wet sand even though it isn't. These products come in a variety of colors and create slime with a unique texture.

KINETIC SAND IN THREE COLORS (LEFT) AND A KINETIC SLIME IN TEAL.

3

BEGINNER SLIMES

ONCE YOU'VE MASTERED
THE TWO BASIC RECIPES IN
CHAPTER 1, THE SIMPLE SLIMES
IN THIS CHAPTER WILL BE
A BREEZE TO MAKE.

SLUSHIE SLIME

THIS SLIME IS STRESS RELIEVING AND CRUNCHY. IT'S SIMILAR TO FISHBOWL SLIME (SEE PAGE 42), BUT THESE BEADS ARE MUCH SMOOTHER AND EASIER TO FIND!

WHAT YOU'LL NEED

Slime-Making Equipment

Large bowl

Measuring cups and spoons

Mixing tool (spoon, spatula, or stir stick)

An airtight container

Ingredients

One batch of Basic Clear Glue Slime (see page 16)

Approximately the same amount of slushie beads (by volume) as slime

Optional

Color additive (see page 24)

1 to 3 drops fragrance oil

VARIATIONS

Gold Glitz = Basic Clear Glue Slime (see page 16) + gold coloring + slushie beads

Pop Rocks = Basic Clear Glue Slime + neon coloring + slushie beads

Elegant = Basic Clear Glue Slime + slushie beads + black microbeads + red glitter

Tropical Crunch = Basic Clear Glue Slime + blue coloring + slushie beads + green glitter

Rose Gold Crunch = Basic Clear Glue Slime + rose gold coloring + slushie beads + green glitter

1.

Make a batch of Basic Clear Glue Slime (see page 16) that's slightly sticky. The slime shouldn't stick everywhere, but it needs to be sticky enough to hold the beads. Add color and/or fragrance oil if you like.

2.

Measure out about the same amount of beads (by volume) as the slime (see A).

3.

Mix the slime with the beads (see B). If the mixture feels too sticky, add a touch more activator. You can add more beads if you prefer a crunchier texture, but if you add too many, they may not all combine with the slime. If the slime is too stiff, dip it in warm water for a few seconds (you'll need adult supervision to do this).

4.

Keep mixing until the beads and the slime are fully combined. Remember: Playing with slime is the best way to mix it!

5.

Store the finished slime in an airtight container so it doesn't dry out.

A.

B.

Yield: Depends on the amount of slime and beads you mix together

FISHBOWL SLIME

THIS CRUNCHY SLIME CAN BE TRICKY TO GET JUST RIGHT, BUT THIS RECIPE WILL HELP SOLVE ALL YOUR FISHBOWL SLIME PROBLEMS!

WHAT YOU'LL NEED

Slime-Making Equipment

Large bowl
Mixing tool (spoon, spatula, or stir stick)
Measuring cups and spoons
An airtight container

Ingredients

One batch of Basic Clear Glue
    Slime (see page 16)
Approximately the same amount
    (by volume) of fishbowl beads
    as slime

Optional

Color additive
1–3 drops of fragrance oil

VARIATIONS

Fruity Fishbowl = Basic Clear Glue Slime (see page 16) + fishbowl beads + fruit polymer clay canes

Fantastic Fishbowl = Basic Clear Glue Slime + gold coloring + fishbowl beads + small foam beads

Strawberry Fishbowl = Basic Clear Glue Slime + pink or red coloring + fishbowl beads + black glitter

Carnival Fishbowl = Basic Clear Glue Slime + fishbowl beads + colorful foam beads + an assortment of glitter

"Finding Nemo" = Basic Clear Glue Slime + orange coloring + fishbowl beads + small, white foam beads + black glitter

1.

Make a batch of Basic Clear Glue Slime (see page 16) that is slightly sticky. The slime shouldn't stick everywhere, but it needs to sticky enough to hold the beads. Add color and/or fragrance oil if you like.

2.

Measure out about the same amount of beads (by volume) as the slime (see A).

3.

Mix the slime with the beads (see B). If the mixture feels too sticky, add a touch more activator. You can add more beads if you prefer a crunchier texture, but if you add too many, they may not all combine with the slime. If the slime is too stiff, dip it in warm water for a few seconds (you'll need adult supervision to do this).

4.

Keep mixing until the beads and the slime are fully combined. Remember: Playing with slime is the best way to mix it!

5.

Store the finished slime in an airtight container so it doesn't dry out.

A.

B.

Yield: Depends on the amount of slime and beads you mix together

DEFLATABLE FLUFFY SLIME

THIS SLIME IS VERY FLUFFY AND STRETCHY. IT CAN BE A MESSY PROCESS TO MAKE, BUT THE FINAL PRODUCT IS WORTH IT! THIS SLIME WILL DEFLATE AFTER 2 TO 4 DAYS BECAUSE SHAVING CREAM IS USED, BUT THE DEFLATED SLIME CAN BE USED TO MAKE ICEBERG SLIME (SEE PAGE 86).

WHAT YOU'LL NEED

Slime-Making Equipment

Large bowl

Measuring cups and spoons

Mixing tool (spoon, spatula, or stir stick)

An airtight container

Ingredients

1 cup (250 ml) white PVA glue (such as Elmer's School Glue)

Approximately ½ cup (125 ml) foaming hand soap

Approximately 1 cup (250 ml) shaving cream

4 tablespoons (60 ml) lotion, divided

An activator (see chart on page 14 for details)

Optional

4 tablespoons (60 ml) cornstarch

Color additive (see page 24)

1 to 3 drops fragrance oil

VARIATIONS

Strawberry Fluff = Deflatable Fluffy Slime + pink coloring + strawberry fragrance oil

Whipped Cream = Deflatable Fluffy Slime + vanilla fragrance oil

Cupcake Batter = Deflatable Fluffy Slime + yellow/beige coloring + vanilla fragrance oil + colorful chunky glitter (a.k.a. "sprinkles")

Vanilla Bean = Deflatable Fluffy Slime + very light yellow coloring + vanilla fragrance oil + fine brown/black glitter

1.

Place the glue in a large bowl. Add the foaming hand soap, shaving cream, cornstarch, and 2 tablespoons (30 ml) of the lotion. Cornstarch isn't necessary, but it helps thicken the mixture, creating a smoother, richer texture. It's fine to only use shaving cream, but the cornstarch makes the slime creamier. Add color and/or fragrance oil if you like. Mix thoroughly.

2.

Add the activator in small amounts, about 1 or 2 tablespoons (15 or 30 ml) at a time (see A). See the guidelines on page 14 for the recommended amounts of each type of activator. Be sure to add only one type of activator to each batch of slime. The measurement isn't exact because different glues activate differently. Also, the amount you add will affect the slime's consistency, and you can adjust it to achieve a consistency you like.

3.

Once the mixture is slightly sticky, start to knead the slime (see B). Dip your fingers in activator before kneading so less slime will stick to your hands. Playing with slime is the best way to mix it fully and achieve the best possible texture.

4.

Add the remaining 2 tablespoons (30 ml) of lotion for extra stretchiness.

5.

Store the finished slime in an airtight container so it doesn't dry out.

Yield: Approximately 18 fluid ounces (560 ml)

A.

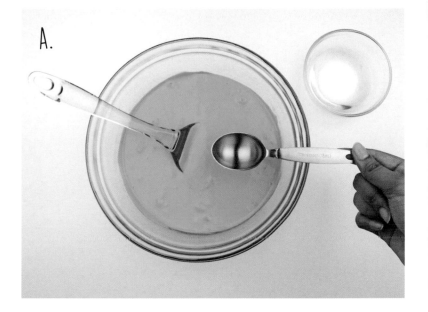

B.

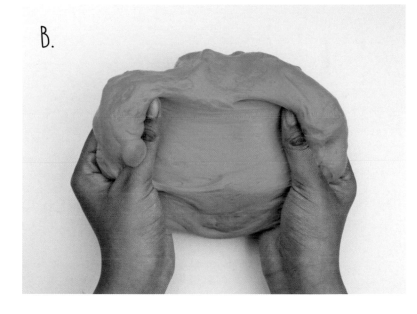

CLAY SLIME

THIS SLIME DOESN'T OOZE THROUGH YOUR FINGERS LIKE REGULAR SLIME. TO ACHIEVE THE PERFECT TEXTURE THAT WON'T BE STICKY, USE ABOUT A THIRD MORE SLIME THAN CLAY.

WHAT YOU'LL NEED

Slime-Making Equipment

Large bowl

Measuring cups and spoons

Mixing tool (spoon, spatula, or stir stick)

An airtight container

Ingredients

One batch of Basic White Glue Slime (see page 14)

Less air-dry clay (by volume) than slime
Note: If you use dense clay, such as Crayola Model Magic, the yield will be less than if using Delight Air Dry Modeling Compound or Hearty Modeling Clay.

Optional

Color additive (see page 24)

1 to 3 drops fragrance oil

Lotion (if needed, to make the slime less stiff)

VARIATIONS

Brownie Slime = Basic White Glue Slime (see page 14) + brown coloring + chocolate fragrance oil + brown clay/white clay

Pineapple Clay Slime = Basic White Glue Slime + yellow coloring + yellow clay/white clay

Abyss Clay Slime = Basic White Glue Slime + black coloring + black clay/white clay

1.

Make a batch of Basic White Glue Slime (see page 14) that's slightly sticky. Optionally, add fragrance oil and/or coloring when making the slime. You can also add these after the slime is made, but it's messier.

2.

Measure out less air-dry clay than slime (see A).

3.

Mix the slime and clay together thoroughly until there are no lumps of clay (see B). The slime should have a smooth texture throughout.

4.

If the mixture is too sticky, add a little more activator. If you prefer a fluffier texture, add a little more clay. If the slime is too stiff, add a little lotion.

5.

Playing with slime is the best way to fully mix the clay and slime together. Keep mixing until the texture is consistent, super creamy, and spreadable!

6.

Store the finished slime in an airtight container so it doesn't dry out.

Yield: Depends on the amount of slime and clay you use

A.

B.

CONFETTI SLIME

THE COLORFUL BEADS GIVE THIS SLIME AN INTERESTING TEXTURE AND AN AMAZING LOOK.

BEGINNER SLIMES

WHAT YOU'LL NEED

Slime-Making Equipment

Large bowl

Measuring cups and spoons

Mixing tool (spoon, spatula, or stir stick)

An airtight container

Ingredients

One batch of Basic White Glue Slime
(see page 14)

However many colorful foam beads you
would like to add to your slime

Optional

Color additive (see page 24)

1 to 3 drops fragrance oil

VARIATIONS

Teal Confetti Slime = Basic White Glue Slime (see page 14)
+ green and blue coloring + large confetti beads

Hot Pink Confetti Slime = Basic White Glue Slime + pink coloring
+ small confetti beads

1.

Make a batch of Basic White Glue Slime (see page 14) that's slightly sticky. Add color and/or fragrance oil if you like. Typically, confetti slime is white, but you can color it if you want.

2.

Measure out the amount of colorful foam beads you would like to use (see A). I like to use an amount equal to about a quarter of the amount of slime (by volume), but you can add however much you want!

A.

3.

Mix the foam beads into the slime (see B). If the mixture is too sticky, add more activator. Remember: Playing with slime is the best way to fully mix the beads and slime together. Also, depending on the beads you buy, the color from the beads may transfer to the slime, making it an off-white. If you do not like this color, add a different coloring, such as pink or blue.

4.

Store the finished slime in an airtight container so the slime doesn't dry out. Note that the foam beads will rise to the top when the slime sits, so you must mix the beads and slime together before each use.

B.

Yield: Depends on the amount of slime and beads you use

SUGAR SLIME

THIS SLIME IS CRUNCHY AND VERY PRETTY. IT LOOKS GREAT WITH GLITTER AND IS FUN TO PLAY WITH. THE TEXTURE IS UNIQUE—YOU WON'T BE ABLE TO PUT IT DOWN!

WHAT YOU'LL NEED

Slime-Making Equipment

Large bowl

Measuring cups and spoons

Mixing tool (spoon, spatula, or stir stick)

An airtight container

Ingredients

One batch of Basic Clear Glue Slime (see page 16)

Approximately the same amount of sugar beads (by volume) as slime

Optional

Color additive (see page 24)

1 to 3 drops of fragrance oil

VARIATIONS

Perfectly Pink Sugar Slime = Basic Clear Glue Slime (see page 16) + pink coloring + sugar beads + pink glitter

Candy Land Sugar Slime = Basic Clear Glue Slime+ yellow coloring + sugar beads + confetti beads

Kaleidoscope Sugar Slime = Basic Clear Glue Slime + multicolor glitter + sugar beads

Intergalactic Sugar Slime = Basic Clear Glue Slime + purple coloring + sugar beads + silver glitter

Penny Crunch = Basic Clear Glue Slime + copper coloring + sugar beads

1.

Make a batch of Basic Clear Glue Slime (see page 16) that's slightly sticky. The slime shouldn't stick everywhere, but it needs to be sticky enough to hold the beads. Add color and/or fragrance oil if you like.

2.

Measure out about the same amount of beads (by volume) as the slime (see A).

3.

Mix the slime with the beads (see B). If the mixture feels too sticky, add a touch more activator. You can add more beads if you prefer a crunchier texture, but if you add too many, they may not all combine with the slime. If the slime is too stiff, dip it in warm water for a few seconds (you'll need adult supervision to do this).

4.

Keep mixing until the beads and the slime are fully combined. Remember: Playing with slime is the best way to mix it!

5.

Store the finished slime in an airtight container so it doesn't dry out.

Yield: Depends on the amount of slime and beads you use

A.

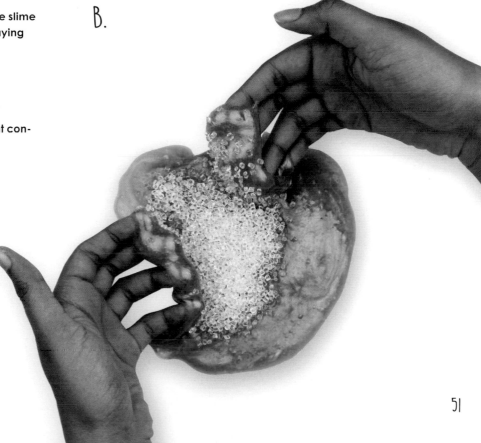

B.

GLITTER BOMB

THIS SLIME GLITTERS AND IS VERY CRUNCHY! IT'S ALSO VERY FUN TO SQUEEZE AND STRETCH. THE AMOUNT OF GLITTER YOU ADD IS COMPLETELY UP TO YOU—THE MORE YOU ADD, THE CRUNCHIER, BUT THE GLITTER MAY FALL OUT. YOU CAN ALSO DO THE SAME THING WITH POLYMER CLAY CANES, BUT THE SLIME WON'T BE AS CRUNCHY.

WHAT YOU'LL NEED

Slime-Making Equipment

Large bowl

Mixing tool (spoon, spatula, or stir stick)

Measuring cups and spoons

An airtight container

Ingredients

One batch of Basic Clear Glue Slime (see page 16)

Approximately two to three times the amount (by volume) of large glitter flakes as slime

Optional

Color additive (see page 24)

1 to 3 drops fragrance oil

VARIATIONS

Fruity Crunch = Basic Clear Glue Slime (see page 16) + polymer clay canes

1.

Make a batch of Basic Clear Glue Slime (see page 16) that's slightly sticky. The slime shouldn't stick everywhere, but it needs to be sticky enough to hold the glitter. Add color and/or fragrance oil if you like.

2.

Measure out about two to three times the amount (by volume) of glitter as slime (see A).

3.

Mix the slime with the glitter (see B). If the mixture feels too sticky, add a touch more activator. You can add more glitter if you prefer a crunchier texture, but if you add too much, it may not mix well with the slime. If the slime is too stiff, dip it in warm water for a few seconds (you'll need adult supervision to do this).

4.

Keep mixing until the glitter and the slime are fully combined. Remember: Playing with slime is the best way to mix it!

5.

Store the finished slime in an airtight container so it doesn't dry out.

A.

B.

Yield: Depends on the amount of slime and glitter you mix together

INTERMEDIATE SLIMES

THIS SECTION HAS INTERESTING SLIMES THAT CAN BE QUITE HARD TO MAKE. BUT BY FOLLOWING THE INSTRUCTIONS AND MAKING EASIER SLIMES BEFORE ATTEMPTING THESE, YOU'LL HAVE NO PROBLEM MAKING THESE SLIMES!

METALLIC SLIME

THIS SLIME IS GORGEOUS! THERE ARE MANY WAYS TO CREATE METALLIC SLIME, AND THIS RECIPE WILL TELL YOU ALL OF THEM.

WHAT YOU'LL NEED

Slime-Making Equipment

Large bowl

Measuring cups and spoons

Mixing tool (spoon, spatula, or stir stick)

An airtight container

Ingredients

One batch of Basic Clear Glue Slime (see page 16)

Pigmented color additive (see Different Ways to Make Metallic Coloring)

Optional

1 to 3 drops of fragrance oil

VARIATIONS

Melted Disco Ball Slime = Basic Clear Glue Slime (see page 16) + silver coloring + holographic silver glitter

Mermaid Lagoon Slime = Basic Clear Glue Slime + pigmented blue coloring + chunky colorful glitter

Pretty in Pink = Basic Clear Glue Slime + pearly coloring + rose gold glitter

Sunken Treasure = Basic Clear Glue Slime + pigmented blue coloring + gold microbeads

24-Carat Gold = Basic Clear Glue Slime + gold coloring

Dazzling Peacock = Basic Clear Glue Slime + pigmented green coloring + chunky blue and silver glitter

1.

Make Basic Clear Glue Slime (see page 16). **(You can't use white glue slime because the metallic colors won't show up.)** Add the coloring (see below for three options) and fragrance oil if you like (see A). **(You can add the fragrance oil after mixing in the color but it's messier.)**

A.

2.

Mix the slime and the coloring together (see B). **You can choose to mix it so the color Is only partially mixed into the slime, or you can mix it until the color is evenly distributed throughout.**

B.

3.

Store the finished slime in an airtight container so it doesn't dry out.

Yield: Depends on the amount of slime you use

DIFFERENT WAYS TO MAKE METALLIC COLORING

There are three different ways to do this:

- **Use pearlescent acrylic paint and a drop of food coloring.** Or, use any metallic-colored acrylic paint.
- **Use eye shadow.** Scrape some of the eye shadow off and add the powder to your slime. This is a great way to use old or unwanted makeup.
- **Use pigments.** This is the best way to create metallic slime because the color is bright and highly pigmented.

JIGGLY SLIME

THIS SLIME JIGGLES AND WOBBLES LIKE NO OTHER SLIME! IT DRIPS THROUGH YOUR FINGERS BUT IS NOT STICKY WHEN MADE PROPERLY.

WHAT YOU'LL NEED

Slime-Making Equipment

Large bowl

Measuring cups and spoons

Mixing tool (spoon, spatula, or stir stick)

An airtight container

Ingredients

1 cup (250 ml) white PVA glue
(such as Elmer's School Glue)

Approximately ½ cup (125 ml) foaming
hand soap

¾ cup (180 ml) warm/hot tap water

An activator (see chart on page
14 for details)

Optional

Color additive (see page 24)

1 to 3 drops of fragrance oil

VARIATIONS

Chocolate Pudding = Jiggly Slime + brown coloring

Banana Cream = Jiggly Slime + yellow coloring

Peaches and Cream = Jiggly Slime + peach coloring + large white foam beads

Rice Pudding = Jiggly Slime + medium foam beads

1.

Place the glue in a large bowl. Add the foaming hand soap and water to the glue. Optionally, add coloring additives and/ or fragrance oil. Mix thoroughly, ensuring the water is fully incorporated (see A). Set aside.

2.

Add activator in small amounts, about 1 or 2 tablespoons (15 or 30 ml) at a time (see B). See the guidelines (on page 14) for the recommended amounts of each type of activator. Be sure to add only one type of activator to each batch of slime. Because of the water, Jiggly Slime requires a little more activator than basic slime. The measurement isn't exact because different glues activate differently. Also, the amount you add will affect the slime's consistency, and you can adjust it to achieve a consistency you like.

3.

Once the mixture is slightly sticky (see C), start to knead the slime. Dip your fingers in activator before kneading so less slime will stick to your hands. Playing with slime is the best way to mix it fully and achieve the best possible texture.

4.

Store the finished slime in an airtight container so it doesn't dry out.

A.

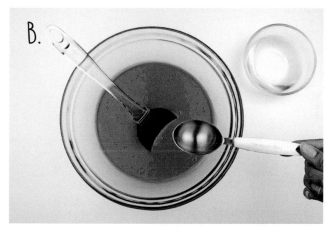

B.

C.

Yield: Approximately 16 fluid ounces (500 ml)

CLEAR GLUE FLOAM

CRUNCHY SLIME IS AMAZING SLIME AND THIS IS THE CRUNCHIEST OF THEM ALL. FOR THIS RECIPE, CLEAR GLUE IS USED TO INCREASE THE FLOAM'S ABILITY TO HOLD FOAM BEADS, MAKING IT CRUNCHIER. FEEL FREE TO USE WHITE GLUE INSTEAD, BUT FOR THE CRUNCHIEST RESULTS, USE CLEAR GLUE.

WHAT YOU'LL NEED

Slime-Making Equipment

Large bowl

Measuring cups and spoons

Mixing tool (spoon, spatula, or stir stick)

An airtight container

Ingredients

One batch of Basic Clear Glue Slime
(see page 16)

The same amount of foam beads (by
volume) as slime

Optional

Color additive (see page 24)

1 to 3 drops of fragrance oil

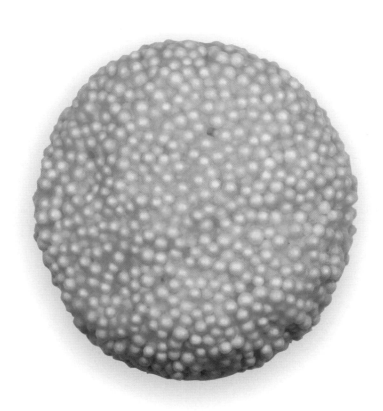

Yield: Depends on the amount of slime and beads you use

INTERMEDIATE SLIMES

1.

Make Basic Clear Glue Slime (see page 16) that's very sticky and stretchy. The slime needs to be able to hold the beads. Optionally, add fragrance oil and/or coloring when making the slime.

2.

Measure out about the same amount of foam beads as slime (see A).

3.

Mix the slime and foam beads together thoroughly (see B). If the mixture is too sticky, add more activator. If you prefer a crunchier texture, add more beads, but, if you add too many, they may fall out. Remember: Playing with slime is the best way to fully mix the beads and slime together.

4.

Store the finsihed slime in an airtight container so it doesn't dry out.

A.

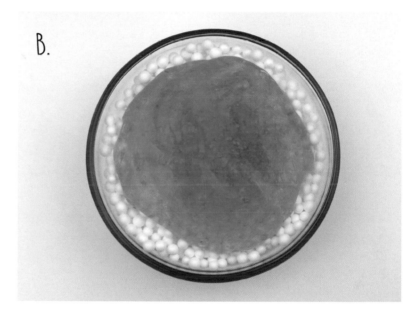

B.

VARIATIONS

Starry Night Floam = Basic Clear Glue Slime (see page 16) + blue coloring + regular foam beads + dark blue glitter

Party Floam = Basic Clear Glue Slime + red coloring + colorful foam beads

Lovely Floam = Basic Clear Glue Slime + pink chunky glitter + small foam beads

Lucky Floam = Basic Clear Glue Slime + green coloring + large foam beads + dark green glitter

Fruit Salad Floam = Basic Clear Glue Slime + small foam beads + fruit polymer clay canes

INTERMEDIATE SLIMES

GEM SLIME

THIS CLEAR GLUE–BASED SLIME IS SOMEHOW FLUFFY YET TRANSLUCENT! THE SPECIAL INGREDIENT IN THIS SLIME CREATES A UNIQUE TEXTURE THAT WILL HAVE YOU NEVER WANTING TO PUT IT DOWN. YOU DON'T NEED TO CRUSH ORBEEZ (POLYMER BEADS THAT ABSORB WATER) OR CUT OPEN A DIAPER FOR THIS SLIME—ALL YOU NEED TO DO IS ADD WATER! CHECK OUT PAGE 35 FOR MORE INFORMATION ON THE MOST IMPORTANT INGREDIENT IN THIS SLIME: SUPER–ABSORBENT POLYMER (SAP).

WHAT YOU'LL NEED

Slime-Making Equipment

Large bowl
Measuring cups and spoons
Mixing tool (spoon, spatula, or stir stick)
An airtight container

Ingredients

One batch of Basic Clear Glue Slime
    (see page 16)
¾ cup (180 ml) Super-Absorbent Polymer
    (by volume when water is added)

Optional

Color additive (see page 24)
1 to 3 drops of fragrance oil

VARIATIONS

Amethyst Gem Slime = Basic Clear Glue Slime (see page 16) + purple coloring + SAP

Diamond Gem Slime = Basic Clear Glue Slime + SAP + fine silver glitter

Bold Gem Slime = Basic Clear Glue Slime + red coloring + SAP

1.

Make Basic Clear Glue Slime (see page 16) that is very sticky and stretchy. The slime needs to be able to hold the SAP. Optionally, add coloring and/or fragrance oil when making the slime (see A).

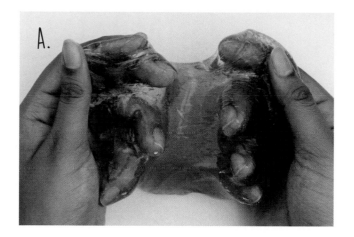

2.

Add water to the SAP according to the package directions and mix well. Measure the correct amount to add to the slime (see B).

3.

Mix the slime and SAP beads together thoroughly (see C). If the mixture is too sticky, add more activator. Remember: Playing with slime is the best way to fully mix the SAP and slime together.

4.

Store the finished slime in an airtight container so it doesn't dry out.

Yield: Approximately 14 fluid ounces (440 ml)

COTTON CANDY SLIME

THIS SLIME IS VERY CRUNCHY AND ADDICTING TO PLAY WITH! IT LOOKS LIKE COTTON CANDY, AND THE PLASTIC FAKE SNOW MAKES FOR A VERY DIFFERENT TEXTURE.

WHAT YOU'LL NEED

Slime-Making Equipment

Large bowl

Measuring cups and spoons

Mixing tool (spoon, spatula, or stir stick)

An airtight container

Ingredients

One batch of Basic White Glue Slime (see page 14)

The same amount of plastic fake snow (by volume) as slime

Optional

Color additive (see page 24)

1 to 3 drops of fragrance oil

VARIATIONS

Tango Cotton Candy Slime = Basic White Glue Slime (see page 14) + pink coloring + fake snow

1.

Make Basic White Glue Slime (see page 14) that's very sticky and stretchy. The slime needs to be able to hold the fake snow. Optionally, add coloring and/or fragrance oil when making the slime.

2.

Measure out about the same amount of fake snow as the slime (see A).

3.

Mix the slime and fake snow together thoroughly (see B). If the mixture is too sticky, add more activator. If you prefer a crunchier texture, add more fake snow, but if you add too much, it may fall out. Remember: Playing with slime is the best way to fully mix the fake snow and slime together.

4.

Store the finished slime an airtight container so it doesn't dry out.

Yield: Depends on the amount of slime and fake snow you use

A.

B.

KINETIC SLIME

THIS SLIME CAN BE TRICKY, BUT IT HAS A VERY INTERESTING TEXTURE!
HAVE FUN PLAYING WITH KINETIC SAND AND MIXING IT INTO SLIME.

WHAT YOU'LL NEED

Slime-Making Equipment

Large bowl

Measuring cups and spoons

Mixing tool (spoon, spatula, or stir stick)

An airtight container

Ingredients

One batch of Basic White Glue Slime
   (see page 14)

The same amount of kinetic sand or Mad
   Mattr (by volume) as slime

¼ cup (60 ml) lotion

Optional

Color additive (see page 24)

1 to 3 drops of fragrance oil

VARIATIONS

Beachy Kinetic Slime = Kinetic Slime + tan coloring + blue glitter
+ gold microbeads

Carnival Kinetic Slime Trio = Swirl these slimes together for an
interesting mixture: red Kinetic Slime + blue Kinetic Slime +
yellow Kinetic Slime

Treasure Hunt Sandbox Slime = Kinetic Slime + tan coloring +
small toy (hide the toy in the slime)

1.

Make Basic White Glue Slime (see page 14) that's very sticky and stretchy. The slime needs to be able to hold the sand. Optionally, add coloring and/or fragrance oil when making the slime.

2.

Measure out about the same amount of kinetic sand as the slime (see A).

3.

Mix the slime and sand together thoroughly (see B). If the mixture is too sticky, add more activator.

4.

Knead in the lotion (see C). Remember: Playing with slime is the best way to fully mix the sand and slime together.

5.

Store the finished slime in an airtight container so it doesn't dry out.

Yield: Depends on the amount of slime and sand you use

A.

B.

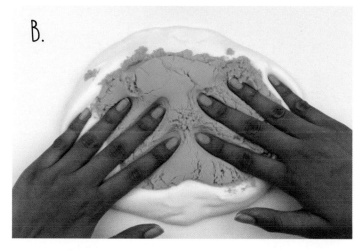

C.

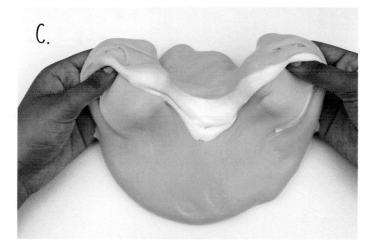

ADVANCED SLIMES

THIS CHAPTER DELVES INTO SLIMES THAT CAN BE CHALLENGING TO MAKE, BUT WITH PATIENCE AND PRACTICE, YOU'LL BE MAKING THEM LIKE A PRO. REMEMBER TO TAKE YOUR TIME AND DON'T GIVE UP!

NON-DEFLATABLE FLUFFY SLIME

THIS RECIPE IS MUCH HARDER TO PERFECT THAN DEFLATABLE FLUFFY SLIME (PAGE 44). IT MIGHT DEFLATE SLIGHTLY BECAUSE IT'S IMPOSSIBLE TO GET PERFECTLY NON-DEFLATABLE SLIME, BUT AFTER PLAYING WITH IT, IT WILL BE AS GOOD AS NEW! THIS COMPLICATED RECIPE HAS MANY INGREDIENTS—EACH HAS A PURPOSE.

WHAT YOU'LL NEED

Slime-Making Equipment

Large bowl

Measuring cups and spoons

Mixing tool (spoon, spatula, or stir stick)

An airtight container

Ingredients

1 cup (250 ml) white PVA glue (such as Elmer's School Glue)

Approximately ½ cup (125 ml) foaming hand soap

Approximately ½ cup (125 ml) shaving cream

4 tablespoons (60 ml) cornstarch

1 tablespoon (15 ml) foaming facial cleanser

4 tablespoons (60 ml) lotion, divided

An activator (see chart on page 14 for details)

¼ cup (60 ml) air-dry clay

Optional

Color additive (see page 24)

1 to 3 drops of fragrance oil

VARIATIONS

Lemon Buttercream = Non-Deflatable Fluffy Slime + yellow coloring

Peach Buttercream = Non-Deflatable Fluffy Slime + peach coloring

Pistachio Buttercream = Non-Deflatable Fluffy Slime + green coloring + fine dark brown glitter

Cherry Buttercream = Non-Deflatable Fluffy Slime + pink/red coloring

Chocolate Buttercream = Non-Deflatable Fluffy Slime + brown coloring

ADVANCED SLIMES

1.

Place the glue in a large bowl. Add the foaming hand soap, shaving cream, cornstarch, foaming facial cleanser, and 2 tablespoons (30 ml) of the lotion to the glue (see A). **Add coloring and/or fragrance oil if you like. Mix thoroughly.**

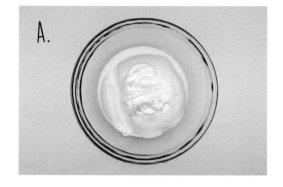

A.

Yield:
Approximately
18 fluid ounces
(560 ml)

2.

Add the activator in small amounts, about 1 or 2 tablespoons (15 or 30 ml) at a time (see B). **See the guidelines on page 14 for the recommended amounts of each type of activator. Be sure to add only one type of activator to each batch of slime. The measurement isn't exact because different glues activate differently. Also, the amount you add will affect the slime's consistency, and you can adjust it to achieve a consistency you like.**

B.

3.

Once the mixture is slightly sticky, start to knead the slime. Knead in the clay (see C). **Dip your fingers in activator before kneading so less slime will stick to your hands. Remember: Playing with slime is the best way to mix it fully and achieve the best possible texture.**

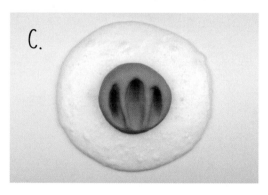

C.

4.

Add the remaining 2 tablespoons (30 ml) of lotion for extra stretchiness (see D).

D.

5.

Store the finished slime in an airtight container so it doesn't dry out.

ADVANCED SLIMES

COMPLETELY CLEAR SLIME

THIS IS THE HARDEST SLIME TO MAKE. PATIENCE IS KEY WHEN MAKING THIS. IF THE SLIME IS NOT STRETCHY ENOUGH WHEN YOU ARE FINISHED, TRY PLACING IT IN SOME WARM WATER FOR A FEW SECONDS AT A TIME. THE ADDED WATER SHOULD ALSO MAKE THE SLIME CLEAR THE AIR BUBBLES FASTER. BUT MAKE SURE YOU DO NOT ADD TOO MUCH WATER, BECAUSE IT CAN IMPACT THE CLEARNESS OF THE SLIME AND EVEN MAKE IT TEAR EASILY INSTEAD OF STRETCHING. PLEASE KEEP IN MIND THAT ANY FRAGRANCE OIL CAN ALSO MAKE YOUR SLIME CLOUDY. ALSO, THE ACTIVATOR YOU DECIDE TO USE MAY NOT CLEAR NICELY, INSTEAD MAKING YOUR SLIME CLOUDY. IN MY EXPERIENCE, USING CONTACT LENS SOLUTION AND BAKING SODA AS AN ACTIVATOR CLEARS THE BEST.

WHAT YOU'LL NEED

Slime-Making Equipment

Large bowl
Measuring cups and spoons
Mixing tool (spoon, spatula, or stir stick)
An airtight container

Ingredients

1 cup (250 ml) clear PVA glue
   (such as Elmer's School Glue)
An activator (see chart on page
   16 for details)

1.

Clean all equipment thoroughly. Place the glue in a large bowl. Pour slowly for the least amount of bubbles (see A).

2.

Add your activator to the glue in small amounts, no more than 2 tablespoons (30 ml) at a time (see B). See the guidelines on page 16 for the recommended amounts of each type of activator. Be sure to add only one type of activator to each batch of slime. For the clearest possible slime, mix slowly. Feel free to mix quickly, but you will need to wait longer for the slime to clear because there will be more bubbles.

3.

Stir the mixture well after adding activator to make sure you don't add too much. Also, the amount you add will affect the slime's consistency, and you can adjust it to achieve a consistency you like. Do not knead the slime. The oils on your hands will transfer to the glue mixture (see C).

4.

Store the finished slime in an airtight container so it doesn't dry out. The slime will clear up in 2 to 5 days, depending on how vigorously you stirred it. When playing with the slime, remember to have clean hands because anything on your hands will be seen in the clear slime.

A.

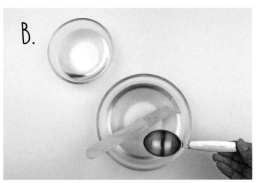

B.

C.

Yield:
Approximately
14 fluid ounces
(420 ml)

VARIATIONS

Detox Water Slime = Basic Clear Glue Slime (see page 16) + a variety of fruit polymer clay canes

Crystal Slime = Basic Clear Glue Slime + fine silver glitter

Lemon Water Slime = Basic Clear Glue Slime + lemon polymer clay canes

BUBBLEGUM SLIME

THIS TYPE OF SLIME IS SIMILAR TO NON-DEFLATABLE FLUFFY SLIME (SEE PAGE 70), BUT THIS ONE IS FLUFFIER AND HOLDS ITS SHAPE BETTER! IT IS PERFECT FOR MAKING SWIRLS BUT WILL DEFLATE BECAUSE OF THE SHAVING CREAM IN THE RECIPE.

WHAT YOU'LL NEED

Slime-Making Equipment

Large bowl

Measuring cups and spoons

Mixing tool (spoon, spatula, or stir stick)

An airtight container

Ingredients

1 cup (250 ml) white PVA glue (such as Elmer's School Glue)

Approximately ½ cup (125 ml) foaming hand soap

Approximately 1 cup (250 ml) shaving cream

5 tablespoons (75 ml) cornstarch

1 tablespoon (15 ml) foaming facial cleanser

4 tablespoons (60 ml) lotion, divided

An activator (see chart on page 14 for details)

Optional

Color additive (see page 24)

1 to 3 drops of fragrance oil

VARIATIONS

Pink Bubblegum Slime = Bubblegum Slime + pink coloring

Mint Bubblegum Slime = Bubblegum Slime + light green coloring

Peppermint Bubblegum Slime = Bubblegum Slime + red glitter

Cinnamon Bubblegum Slime = Bubblegum Slime + fine brown glitter

1.

Place the glue in a large bowl. Add the foaming hand soap, shaving cream, cornstarch, foaming facial cleanser, and 2 tablespoons (30 ml) of lotion to the glue. Add color and/or fragrance oil if you like (see A). **Mix thoroughly.**

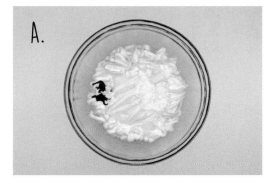

A.

Yield:
Approximately
20 fluid ounces
(625 ml)

2.

Add activator in small amounts, about 1 or 2 tablespoons (15 or 30 ml) at a time (see B). **See the guidelines on page 14 for the recommended amounts of each type of activator. Be sure to add only one type of activator to each batch of slime. The measurement isn't exact because different glues activate differently. Also, the amount you add will affect the slime's consistency, and you can adjust it to achieve a consistency you like.**

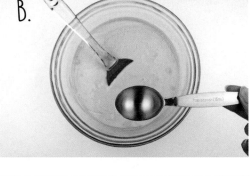

B.

3.

Once the mixture is slightly sticky, start to knead the slime (see C). Dip your fingers in activator before kneading so less slime will stick to your hands. Remember: Playing with slime is the best way to mix it fully and achieve the best possible texture.

C.

4.

Add the remaining 2 tablespoons (30 ml) lotion for extra stretchiness (see D).

5.

Store the finished slime in an airtight container so it doesn't dry out.

D.

BUTTER SLIME

THIS SLIME ISN'T ACTUALLY MADE WITH BUTTER, BUT LOOKS LIKE IT! IT'S SOFT, FLUFFY, AND VERY FUN TO SQUEEZE.

WHAT YOU'LL NEED

Slime-Making Equipment

Large bowl

Mixing tool (spoon, spatula, or stir stick)

Measuring cups and spoons

An airtight container

Ingredients

One batch of Basic White Glue Slime (see page 14)

Approximately the same amount (by volume) of air-dry clay as slime

Optional

Color additive (see page 24)

1 to 3 drops of fragrance oil

Lotion (if needed; to make the slime less stiff)

Cornstarch (if needed; to make the slime thicker)

AIR-DRY CLAYS FOR MAKING BUTTER SLIME

Daiso Soft Clay, a Japanese product, is the best air-dry clay for making butter slime, but it can be difficult to find. Other air-dry clays, such as Crayola Model Magic, Delight Air Dry Modeling Compound (the brand I used to make the butter slime shown), and Hearty Super Lightweight Modeling Clay, will also work if you add lotion to your slime.

VARIATIONS

Cookie Dough = Butter Slime + tan coloring + baked pieces of brown polymer clay

Strawberry Cream Cheese = Butter Slime + pink coloring

ADVANCED SLIMES

1.

Make a batch of Basic White Glue Slime (see page 14) that's slightly sticky. Add color and/or fragrance oil if you like.

2.

Measure out about the same amount of air-dry clay as slime (see A).

3.

Mix the slime and clay together thoroughly until there are no lumps of clay. The slime should have a smooth texture throughout (see B).

4.

If the mixture is too sticky, add a little more activator. If you prefer a fluffier texture, add a little more clay. If the slime is too stiff, add a little lotion. Add a little cornstarch for a thicker texture.

5.

Playing with slime is the best way to fully mix the clay and slime together. Keep mixing until the texture is consistent, super creamy, and spreadable!

6.

Store the finished slime in an airtight container so it doesn't dry out.

A.

B.

Yield: Depends on the amount of slime and clay you use.

SOFT SERVE SLIME

THIS MATTE SLIME IS SOOTHING AND RELAXING TO PLAY WITH, AND IT'S FUN TO SPREAD. THIS SLIME WILL OOZE THROUGH YOUR FINGERS BUT IT'S VERY EASY TO GET OFF YOUR HANDS.

WHAT YOU'LL NEED

Slime-Making Equipment

Large bowl

Measuring cups and spoons

Mixing tool (spoon, spatula, or stir stick)

An airtight container

Ingredients

1 cup (250 ml) white PVA glue (such as Elmer's School Glue)

Approximately ½ cup (125 ml) foaming hand soap

2 cups (500 ml) cornstarch, divided

4 tablespoons (60 ml) lotion, divided

An activator (see chart on page 14 for details)

Optional

Color additive (see page 24)

1 to 3 drops of fragrance oil

VARIATIONS

Peachy Dreams = Soft Serve Slime + red and yellow coloring

Strawberry Dreams = Soft Serve Slime + pink coloring

Marshmallow Dreams = Soft Serve Slime + marshmallow fragrance oil

Honeydew Dreams = Soft Serve Slime + green coloring

Blueberry Dreams = Soft Serve Slime + blue coloring

1.

Place the glue in a large bowl. Add the foaming hand soap, 1 cup (250 ml) of the cornstarch, and 2 tablespoons (30 ml) of the lotion to the glue. Add color and/or fragrance oil if you like (see A). **Mix thoroughly.**

A.

Yield:
Approximately
20 fluid ounces
(645 ml)

2.

Add activator in small amounts, about 1 or 2 tablespoons (15 or 30 ml) at a time (see B). **See the guidelines on page 14 for the recommended amounts of each type of activator. Be sure to add only one type of activator to each batch of slime. The measurement isn't exact because different glues activate differently. Also, the amount you add will affect the slime's consistency, and you can adjust it to achieve a consistency you like.**

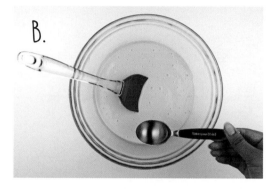

B.

3.

Once the mixture is slightly sticky, start to knead the slime (see C). Dip your fingers in activator before kneading so less slime will stick to your hands. **Remember: Playing with slime is the best way to mix it fully and achieve the best possible texture.**

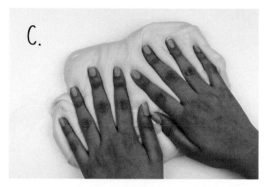

C.

4.

Add up to the remaining 1 cup (125 g) cornstarch if the slime isn't matte enough for your liking. Add the remaining 2 tablespoons (30 ml) lotion for extra stretchiness (see D).

D.

5.

Store the finished slime in an airtight container so it doesn't dry out.

SLIMES IN ACTION

THIS CHAPTER IS ALL ABOUT TEMPORARY USES FOR SLIME. FOR VARYING PERIODS OF TIME, THE SLIME WILL LOOK INTERESTING AND CREATE A UNIQUE LOOK THAT CAN BE FUN TO PLAY WITH.

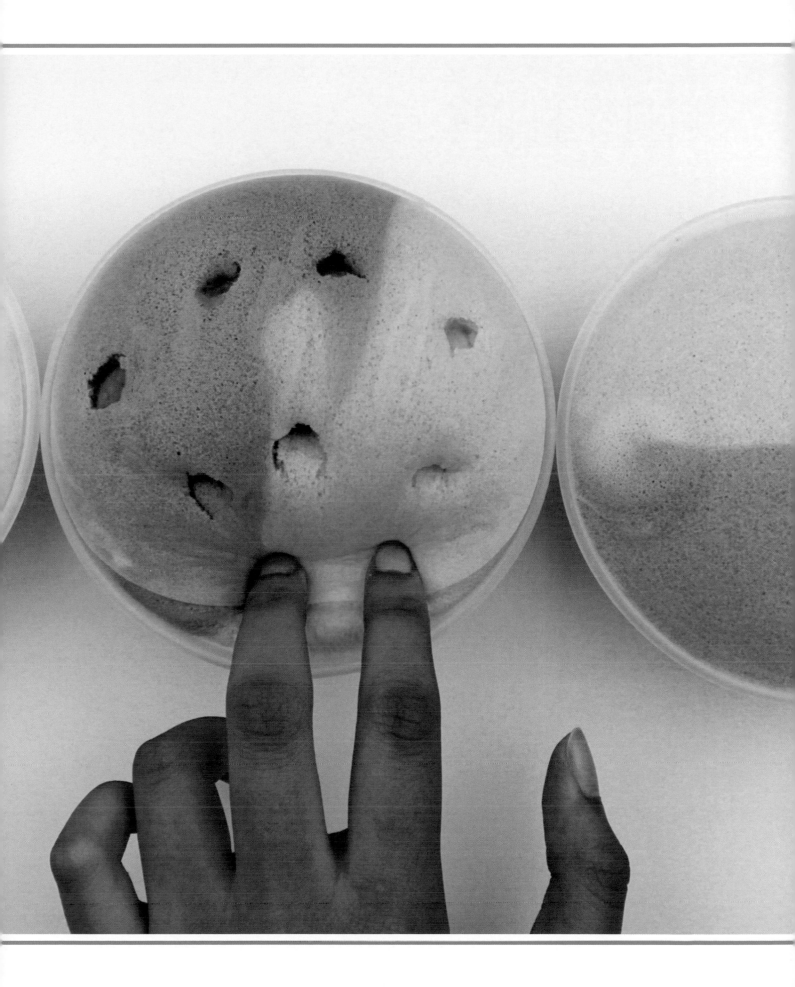

BUBBLY SLIME

THERE ARE MANY DIFFERENT WAYS TO ACHIEVE BUBBLY SLIME!

Let Sit Overnight

Almost any slime you make, when left to sit overnight, will form bubbles because when making it, air bubbles are formed from the stirring. These bubbles will rise to the top of whatever covered container you store it in. However, you can achieve bubblier slime than this. I have found that thicker and more bubbles come from white glue–based slimes, but clear glue bubbles can be very crunchy. For clear glue–based bubbly slime, simply mix vigorously when making it then let it sit overnight. You can also do this with white glue slimes.

A CLEAR GLUE–BASED SLIME (ABOVE) AND A WHITE GLUE–BASED SLIME WHOSE BUBBLES FORMED WHEN THEY WERE LEFT TO SIT OVERNIGHT.

SLIMES IN ACTION

Here are two ways to make even bubblier white glue–based slimes:

Method 1

Use the Basic White Glue Slime recipe on page 14, but instead of using ½ cup (125 ml) of foaming hand soap, use 2 cups (500 ml) or more (by volume). Let the slime sit for 1 to 2 days in an airtight container and crisp bubbles will form.

Method 2

The second way is to use the Basic White Glue Slime recipe on page 14, and add 2 to 3 cups (500 to 750 ml) shaving cream (by volume). Let the slime sit for 1 to 2 days in an airtight container and crisp bubbles will form. This creates thick bubbles that make more of a "fizzy" sound, less of a "crunchy" sound. You might find that your bubbles are very sticky when using this method. The key to avoiding sticky bubbles is to make sure the slime itself is not sticky at all when you put it in the container, meaning you may need to add more activator.

Please note that all of these bubbly slimes are temporary—once the bubbles have been popped, you'll need to repeat the process by adding shaving cream or foaming hand soap to the slime. After a few times, the slime will stop becoming bubbly and may even liquefy. At that point, you can create Iceberg Slime (see page 86).

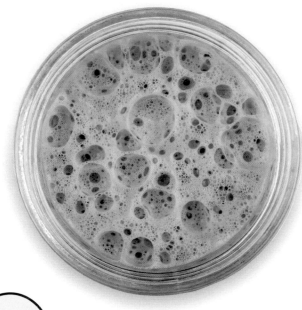

AVALANCHE SLIME

THIS IS A TEMPORARY, INTERESTING—LOOKING SLIME. YOU CAN ADD GLITTER, MICROBEADS, AND OTHER ADDITIVES IF YOU WOULD LIKE TO MAKE YOUR SLIME LOOK MORE EXCITING. CHECK OUT CHAPTER 2 FOR MORE ADDITIVES.

SLIMES IN ACTION

To create Avalanche Slime, you'll need both Basic White Glue Slime (see page 14) and Basic Clear Glue Slime (see page 16).

1.

Fill half a container with Basic Clear Glue Slime. You can have as many colors as you would like (see A).

2.

Fill the rest of the container with Basic White Glue Slime (see B).

3.

Poke the slime three to six times, but not more than that or the slime will mix too much (see C). Let the slime sit for 1 or 2 days, and you'll have Avalanche Slime!

Please note that once you mix the slimes you won't be able to unmix them—they'll become one, single new slime.

A.

B.

C.

ICEBERG SLIME

THIS SLIME MAKES A VERY SATISFYING SIZZLING OR FIZZY SOUND AND IS SO FUN TO MAKE AND PLAY WITH. IT'S ALSO A GREAT WAY TO MAKE USE OF OLD SLIME.

SLIMES IN ACTION

1.

Take 1 cup (250 ml) old Basic White Glue Slime (see page 14) that's slightly sticky and add four times the amount of shaving cream to it, by volume, so about 4 cups (1000 ml). I find sticky slime works well when making Iceberg Slime, but you may need to add a little activator. Also add in ¼ to ½ cup (60 to 125 ml) cornstarch (see A). Note that if you use two different colors of slime, divide the shaving cream and cornstarch in half and add to each color separately.

2.

Place it in a large bowl, preferably made of glass or metal (see B). Let this sit out for 3 or 4 days until a thick layer of slime has dried on the top. Do not touch the slime during this time.

3.

Once the layer has formed (see C), poke it. If you would like, peel the top, dried layer off or mix it back into the slime. It will eventually dissolve back into the slime. You can make Iceberg Slime again by adding more shaving cream and cornstarch. This should work for a few more times, but eventually the slime will fully liquefy.

If you don't have any old Basic White Glue Slime, just make a new batch and follow the same steps.

A.

B.

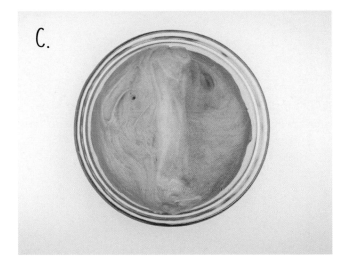

C.

OMBRÉ SLIME

THIS SLIME IS VERY PRETTY AND SIMPLE TO ACHIEVE!

1.

Take two different colors of slime and then place them next to each other in an airtight container (see A).

2.

Let them sit for a few days and they should blend together, creating a gorgeous ombré (see B)! Use the same type of slime for best results.

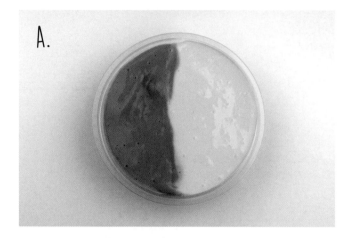

A.

B.

SLIMES IN ACTION

Jiggly Slime

I've found that Jiggly Slime (see page 58) blends the fastest because there is so much water in it. You only need to wait overnight.

Thicker Slimes

Thicker slimes like Butter Slime (see page 76) take longer to blend, so if you're impatient, use Jiggly Slime!

Add-ins

You can add glitter, microbeads, and other additives if you would like to make your slime look more interesting. Check out Chapter 2 for more additives.

SWIRLING SLIME

DESPITE WHAT YOU MAY THINK, SWIRLING SLIME CAN BE DIFFICULT TO MAKE. IT MIGHT REQUIRE SOME PRACTICE, AND NOT ALL SLIMES WILL SWIRL.

For example, Jiggly Slime (see page 58) will not swirl well, whereas Clay Slime (see page 46) will. For best results, use a thick slime that holds its shape.

SLIMES IN ACTION

A.

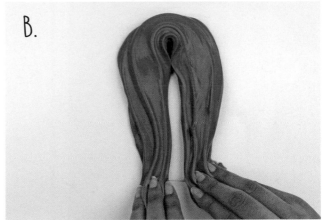

B.

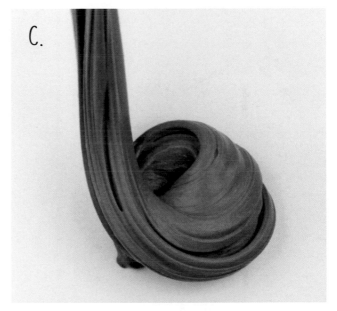

C.

D.

1.

To swirl slime, first pick it up (see A). Stretch it and then fold it so the two ends meet. Repeat this process several times until you are satisfied with the shape of the slime. I like when the lines formed are smooth (see B).

2.

You can either place the end of the slime that is not in your hand on the table or in your other hand. Wrap the slime around itself (see C).

3.

Tuck the end under the slime (see D). You must work quickly because the slime will ooze and lose the shape of the swirl.

This is a fun way to play with your slime because squeezing the swirl can create popping sounds. It also looks very pretty.

7

PLAYING WITH AND USING SLIME

IN THIS CHAPTER, YOU'LL LEARN ALL ABOUT HOW TO USE SLIME IN A VARIETY OF DIFFERENT WAYS, LIKE CREATING SLIME THAT LOOKS JUST LIKE FOOD AND HOW TO MAKE A STRESS BALL!

SATISFYING SLIME SOUNDS

DIFFERENT SLIMES MAKE DIFFERENT SOUNDS, AS YOU MAY HAVE HEARD WHEN WATCHING VIDEOS OF SLIME. HERE'S A GUIDE TO MAKING THESE DIFFERENT SOUNDS.

PLAYING WITH AND USING SLIME

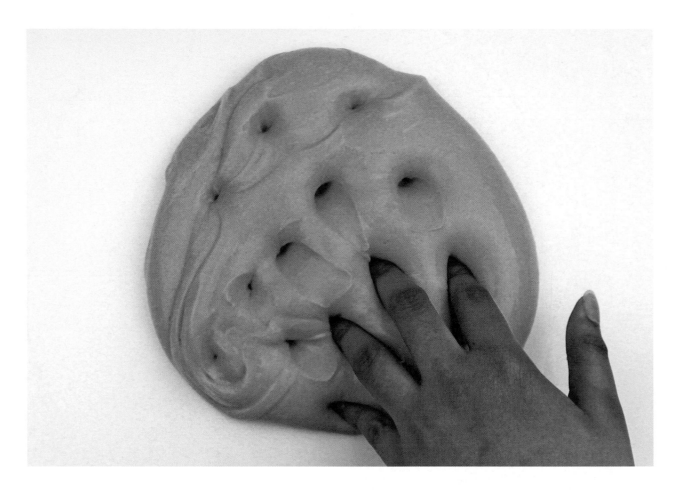

Poking

This is one of the most popular things to do with slime. Glossy slimes work best for this, but of course, you can poke any slime. Also, let your slime sit for a day or two after making it because once the bubbles rise to the top and pop, the slime becomes glossier and makes better poking sounds. You can add baby oil for louder sounds.

POKING SLIME IS VERY FUN AND MAKES INTERESTING SOUNDS.

Popping

There are three main ways to create a popping sound: swirling, what I call the "stretch and drop," and slime "pressing." These all create bubbles that pop when you squeeze the slime.

Swirling. This is explained in depth on page 90. The act of stretching and folding the slime results in bubbles and they all pop when you squeeze the swirl.

The "Stretch and Drop." This isn't the most visually appealing way to create bubbles, but it works well! Stretch the slime thinly and then drop it onto a table. Repeat this process several times, taking care not to pop the existing bubbles. Once you're happy, squeeze it as much as you would like and then do it all over again. You can also do this and then swirl the slime if you want the slime to be more visually appealing, but stretching and folding the slime to swirl it will pop some of the bubbles.

Pressing. This is a trend where you take anything like a badminton/tennis racket or a rack and press it into the slime. You lift it up and then either take the slime off or press the racket/rack back down into the slime. This creates many bubbles that are very fun to pop, but just make sure you use something you do not mind getting slime on or something that is not used for food.

THE FINAL STEP IN THE "STRETCH AND DROP" POPPING TECHNIQUE.

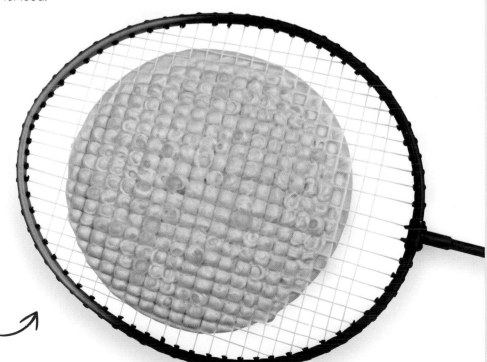

PRESSING SLIME WITH A BADMINTON RACKET.

Sizzle

Freshly made Butter Slime (see page 76) can "sizzle" when you squish it!

Crunch

There is the typical crunch floam makes and there is a "soft" crunch and "fishbowl" crunch. A soft crunch is a crunchy slime that is not overly crunchy; it is a quieter, almost soothing sound. Usually white glue–based slimes have a soft crunch because it is hard to make it very crunchy. Clear glue floam made with very small foam beads can also have a soft crunch. Fishbowl crunch is basically the sound Fishbowl Slime (see page 42) and any other slime with similar beads (Slushie, Sugar, etc.) makes. Some describe it as a "watery" sound.

LISTEN TO YOUR
BUTTER SLIME SIZZLE!

"SOFT CRUNCH" (ABOVE) AND "FISHBOWL CRUNCH" ARE BOTH VERY SATISFYING SOUNDS!

DIY SLIME STRESS BALL

WHETHER YOU HAVE A BIG TEST COMING UP OR JUST WANT TO FIDGET WHILE WATCHING TELEVISION, THIS IS THE TOY FOR YOU!

WHAT YOU'LL NEED

Slime-Making Equipment

Large bowl

Measuring cups and spoons

Mixing tool (spoon, spatula, or stir stick)

An airtight container

Ingredients

Enough Basic White Glue Slime
(page 14) to fill the balloon

Balloon

Fishnet stockings

Optional

Funnel or water bottle

1.

Make a batch of Basic White Glue Slime (see page 14).

2.

Put the slime into the balloon and then tie off the end. You can use a funnel that you do not use for food or make your own using a water bottle (see A). To do this, carefully cut off the bottom of the water bottle using scissors. (Please have a parent do this, as the plastic can be sharp.)

A.

3.

Place the balloon filled with slime in the fishnet stockings where your feet would usually go (see B).

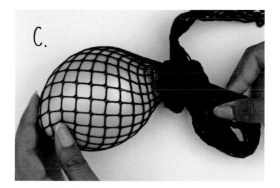

B.

4.

Cut off the rest of the stocking and tie the end (see C).

C.

5.

Squish away (see D)!

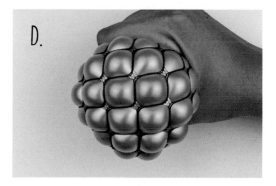

D.

SLIME FOOD REPLICAS

THERE ARE COUNTLESS DIFFERENT WAYS TO MAKE SLIME LOOK LIKE FOOD! YOU CAN ALSO SCENT SLIME USING FRAGRANCE OILS SO IT WILL ACTUALLY SMELL LIKE THE FOOD YOU'RE TRYING TO REPLICATE. HERE ARE A FEW EXAMPLES.

PLAYING WITH AND USING SLIME

Ice Cream

Color Basic White Glue Slime (see page 14) with your favorite "flavor" and add faux sprinkles.

SAFETY NOTE!

Make sure to label your food replicas as slime so no one will eat them!

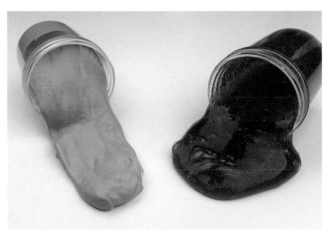

Strawberry Jam

Make Basic Clear Glue Slime (see page 16). Color this slime dark red and add dark red glitter. Put it in a jam jar. You can also make blueberry jam, orange marmalade, and many more.

Peanut Butter and Jelly

Make peanut butter–colored Butter Slime (see page 70) for the "peanut butter." Make the "jelly" out of Basic Clear Glue Slime (see page 16) colored purple.

YOU CAN ALSO MAKE SLIME "TOAST" TO SPREAD YOUR SLIME JAM AND PB3J ON!

Popcorn

Make Basic White Glue Slime (see page 14). Color it yellow and add chunks of crushed Styrofoam or large foam beads.

Chocolate Chip Cookies and Milk

Make tan Butter Slime (see page 76). Make "chocolate chips" out of brown polymer clay. Mix the two together. For the "milk," make white Jiggly Slime (see page 58).

Apple Pie

Take a pie tin and fill it with red Basic White Glue Slime (see page 14) **(see A).** Make tan-colored Basic White Glue Slime for the crust. Surround the edge of the pie tin with the crust. You can simply lay a sheet of "crust" on top of the pie, or you can form it into strips and create a lattice (over-and-under) pattern **(see B).**

A.

B.

DECORATIVE SLIME JARS

DO YOU HAVE SLIME AND NEED AN IDEA FOR DISPLAYING IT? MAKING A CUTE JAR TO STORE IT IN WILL GIVE YOUR DÉCOR A TOUCH OF SLIME!

WHAT YOU'LL NEED

Airtight Mason jar
Enough Basic White Glue Slime
　(page 14) to fill the jar

SLIME SHIFT

Over time, the different color slimes will mix together and become one color. These changes are fun to watch, especially if there are different add-ins in each layer.

SLIME JAR VARIATION

Frozen Rose Snow Globe = red butter slime sculpted into a rose + green butter slime sculpted into a leaf + surrounded by clear glue slime

1.

Make a batch of Basic White Glue Slime (see page 14).

2.

Divide the slime into equal portions. Add a different color of acrylic paint to each (see A).

3.

Mix the paint into each portion of slime (see B).

4.

Layer the slime in the jar. See Ombré Slime (page 88) for tips on layering slime.

5.

Secure the lid of the container so the slime won't dry out. Occasionally play with the slime and add activator so it doesn't liquify.

6.

Get creative! Decorate the jar by using acrylic paints to paint it with a cute Kawaii face and then glue on googly eyes and ribbon with a low-temperature glue gun (you'll need an adult's help to use one). I used Basic White Glue Slime to make my layers, but you can use any slime recipe in this book! See opposite and pages 106-107 for other variations.

A.

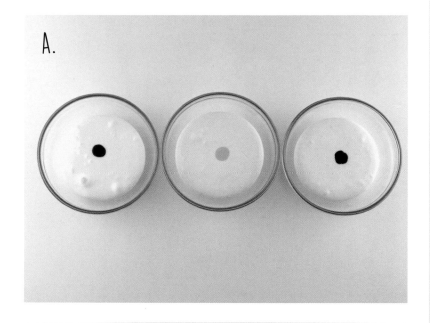

B.

Marble

Swirl any type of different colored slimes and place into a container.

Day at the Beach

Press tan Butter Slime (see page 76) in to the bottom of a container. Fill with blue Clear Glue Slime (see page 16) and add in some seashells.

Layers

Layer slimes together to create an interesting, colorful look.

I Heart You

Shape red Butter Slime (see page 76) into a heart. Surround it with glossy black slime.

DRAWING ON SLIME

MAKE A BATCH OF BASIC WHITE GLUE SLIME (SEE PAGE 14). ADD THREE TO FOUR TIMES THE AMOUNT OF CORNSTARCH (BY VOLUME) AS SLIME. MIX IT TOGETHER THOROUGHLY. NOW YOU WILL BE ABLE TO TAKE A MARKER AND COLOR ON THE SLIME.

I like to use Crayola markers with the large tip. It's very interesting to see how the drawings change as the slime oozes. Afterward, you can mix up your slime and see what new color is formed. You can store it in an airtight container and use it another time to create a new drawing. There are a variety of things that you can draw; see below and opposite for some ideas.

Doodles

Patterns

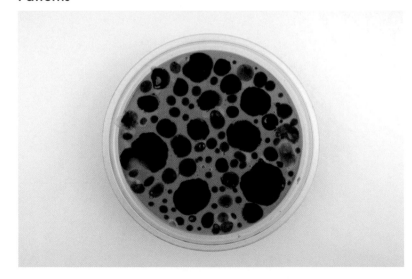

PLAYING WITH AND USING SLIME

Flowers

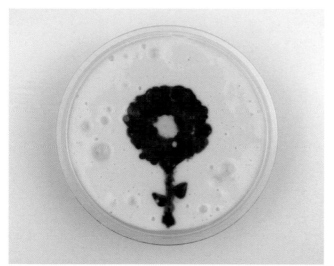

Night Sky

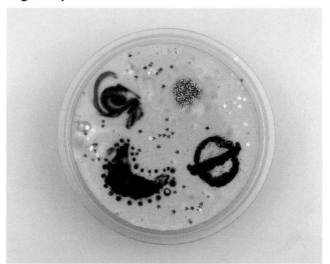

Landscapes

Butterflies

RESOURCES

I SHOP FOR MY SLIME-MAKING SUPPLIES AT CRAFT STORES, DOLLAR STORES, IN THE ARTS AND CRAFTS SECTIONS OF MASS MERCHANDISERS, STORES, AND ONLINE. BELOW IS A LIST OF SOME OF THE BRANDS I LIKE TO USE.

Basic Slime Ingredients

Clean & Clear Essentials Foaming Facial Cleanser
www.cleanandclear.ca/products/facial-cleansers/
essentials-foaming-facial-cleanser

Elmer's Glue
http://elmers.com/

Renu Fresh Multi-Purpose Contact Lens Cleaning Solution
www.renu.com/

Sta-Flo Liquid Starch
www.purex.com/products/laundry-enhancers/
sta-flo-liquid-starch/

Tide Free and Gentle Liquid Laundry Detergent
https://tide.ca/en-ca/shop/type/liquid/
tide-free-and-gentle-liquid

Add-ins

Crayola Model Magic
www.crayola.ca/things-to-do/how-to-landing/
model-magic.aspx

Delight Air Dry Modeling Compound
www.paperclay.com/product.htm

FloraCraft Winter Snow
www.floracraft.com/products/styrofoam/shred/
winter-snow/

Hearty Air Dry Clay
https://activaproducts.com/collections/air-dry-clay

Insta-Snow (Super-Absorbent Polymer)
www.instasnow.com/

Kinetic Sand
http://kineticsand.com/?loc=en_CA

Pearl Ex Pigments
www.jacquardproducts.com/pearl-ex-pigments.html

WABA Fun Mad Mattr
http://kodokids.com/mad-mattr

These products are available at Michaels:

Ashland Diamond Filler
Ashland Clear Decorative Filler
Recollections Glitter
Recollections Microbeads

You can find these products online:

Daiso Soft Clay
Martha Stewart Flocking Powder

Connect with Me!

Instagram: @craftyslimecreator
Etsy: craftedbyalyssaj

ABOUT THE AUTHOR

ALYSSA JAGAN IS ALSO KNOWN AS ALYSSA OF @CRAFTYSLIMECREATOR.

The popular Instagram slimer is a 16-year-old high school student who lives with her family in Toronto. Alyssa posts three slime videos to her main Instagram account every day and sells her slime creations on Etsy. Visit her on Instagram at @CraftySlimeCreator; on YouTube at Alyssa J; and on Etsy at CraftedbyAlyssaJ.

INDEX

BEDFORD FREE PUBLIC LIBRARY
7 Mudge Way
Bedford, MA 07730-2158